The Wild Life of LIZARDS

By Camilla de la Bédoyère

WINDMILL
BOOKS

THE WILD SIDE

Published in 2015 by **WINDMILL BOOKS**, an Imprint of Rosen Publishing
29 East 21ˢᵗ Street, New York, NY 10010

© 2015 Miles Kelly Publishing

Publishing Director: Belinda Gallagher
Creative Director: Jo Cowan
Editorial Director: Rosie Neave
Senior Editor: Claire Philip
Designers: Jo Cowan, Venita Kidwai
Image Manager: Liberty Newton
Production Manager: Elizabeth Collins
Reprographics: Stephan Davis, Thom Allaway

ACKNOWLEDGEMENTS

The publishers would like to thank Mike Foster (Maltings Partnership), Joe Jones, and Richard Watson (Bright Agency) for the
illustrations they contributed to this book. All other artwork from the Miles Kelly Artwork Bank.

The publishers would like to thank the following sources for the use of their photographs: t = top, b = bottom, l = left,
r = right, c = center, bg = background, rt = repeated throughout. **Cover** (front) Cathy Keifer/Shutterstock, (back)
ZSSD/Minden Pictures/FLPA; Joke panel (rt) Tropinina Olga. **Corbis** 10 Theo Allofs; 11 Stuart Westmorland
Photography/Image Source. **FLPA** 6 Emanuele Biggi; 13 Tui De Roy/Minden Pictures; 14 Cyril Ruoso/Minden Pictures; 18
Chris Mattison; 22 Piotr Naskrecki/Minden Pictures. **Nature Picture Library** 13 Bence Mate; 19 Bruce Davidson; 20
Dave Watts. **Shutterstock** Speech bubbles (rt) tachyglossus; Heading panel (rt) Ryan M. Bolton; Joke panel (rt) Tropinina
Olga; Learn a Word panel (rt) donatas1205; Learn a Word cartoon (rt) RAStudio; 1 Cathy Keifer/Shutterstock; 3 Irina oxilixo
Danilova; 4–5 Eric Isselée, 5(t) Eric Isselée, (b) Mammut Vision; 7(t) Eduard Kyslynskyy, (b) Uryadnikov Sergey; 8(b/g) Denis
Kholyavin, (Brush stroke) Ambient ideas, (panel) Anna Ts; (music notes) Tracie Andrews; 9(t–b) Joan Kerrigan, Alhovik,
TheBlackRhino; 11(b) Joe Farah; 12 Melissa Brandes; 15(t) Brandon Alms; 16–17(b/g) David M. Schrader; 16(l–r panels)
LittleRambo, alexcoolok, (b) verdeskerde; 17(panel) LittleRambo, (c) mirabile, (bl) Sergey Mikhaylov, 21 Manja.

LIBRARY OF CONGRESS CATALOGING-IN-PUBLICATION DATA

De la Bédoyère, Camilla, author.
 The wild life of lizards / Camilla de la Bedoyere.
     pages cm. — (The wild side)
 Includes index.
 ISBN 978-1-4777-5495-5 (pbk.)
 ISBN 978-1-4777-5496-2 (6 pack)
 ISBN 978-1-4777-5494-8 (library binding)
 1. Lizards—Juvenile literature. I. Title.
 QL666.L2D45 2015
 597.95—dc23
                    2014027096

Manufactured in the United States of America

CPSIA Compliance Information: Batch #CW15WM: For Further Information contact Rosen Publishing, New York, New York at 1-800-237-9932

Contents

I am a lizard!

I am a type of animal called a reptile. We have dry, scaly skin and are cold-blooded. This means we need heat from the Sun to warm up our bodies.

Ear

•Long tail

There are more than 5,000 different types of lizards!

Q. Why is it easy to weigh a lizard?

A. Because they always carry scales!

• • • • • • Dry, scaly skin

• • • • • Four legs

• • • • Sharp claws

Scaly cousins

Lizards, snakes and alligators all belong to the reptile family. Turtles and tortoises are also in the same group.

Snake

Snakes have long, thin bodies with no legs. Some are deadly.

Huge alligators and crocodiles have big jaws and long, sharp teeth.

Alligator

What do you eat?

I eat juicy bugs!

I sneak up on my prey and grab it with my claws or mouth. I use my teeth to chew.

Flying gecko

LEARN A WORD:

prey
An animal that is hunted for food by other animals.

Super sticky tongue

A chameleon shoots out its tongue to catch insects. Then it pulls the bug back into its open mouth and eats it.

Long tongue

Plant eaters

A few types of lizards eat plants. They feed on leaves, fruit and flowers.

Q. Why are lizards always happy?

A. They eat whatever bugs them!

Land iguana

Activity time

Get ready to make and do!

Draw me!

YOU WILL NEED: pencils · paper

1. Draw two ovals for the head and body.

2. Now draw the lizard's legs, feet, tail and eyes.

3. Draw toes and claws on the feet. Give the lizard a tongue. Lastly, add dots to the eyes.

Frozen lizards

With a few friends, play some music in a large room. When the music plays, crawl like a lizard. When the music stops, freeze. The winner is the last to move! Take turns to be in charge of the music.

Now color me in and give me a name!

8

Wild art

YOU WILL NEED:
paper · colored pencils or paints · scissors

Ask for help!

HERE'S HOW:
Aboriginal artists of Australia decorate their lizard pictures with lots of different patterns. Draw some lizard outlines and decorate each one with dots, bands, stripes, and circles. Add a colorful pattern around the lizard.

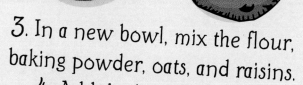

Bug biscuits

Ask for help!

YOU WILL NEED:
¼ cup butter
¼ cup granulated sugar
1 tbsp honey · 1 egg
¼ cup plain flour
1 tsp baking powder
⅓ cup oats · ¼ cup raisins

HERE'S HOW:
1. Turn on oven to 350°F.
2. In a bowl, beat the butter and sugar together, then beat in the honey and the egg.

3. In a new bowl, mix the flour, baking powder, oats, and raisins.
4. Add the butter mixture to the flour mixture.
5. Dollop spoonfuls onto a greased baking sheet and bake for 10–12 minutes.

Where do you live?

I live in warm places.

Lizards live around the world in areas where the weather is warm, such as deserts. The heat warms up our blood to give us energy.

Thorny devil

In the jungle

Lots of lizards live in hot and steamy rainforests. They climb up into the trees, looking for places to hide and food to eat.

Black iguana

Q. What do hip-hop lizards call themselves?

A. Rap-tiles!

Blue collared lizard

Sun seeker

Lizards sunbathe to soak up warmth. This is called basking. If they get too hot they move into the shade.

How do you move?

Climbing

I can run fast and climb upside down!

The feet of some lizards, such as geckos, are very sticky. We can run along rocks, up trees and under branches.

Running on water

Basilisk lizards are amazing reptiles. Their long toes and tails help them run across water.

Running

Q. Why did the lizard cross the road?

A. To prove he wasn't a chicken!

Big swimmer

Marine iguanas are large lizards that swim in the sea. They feed on seaweed.

Swimming

How big are you?

I am the biggest lizard in the world!

I am a huge, heavy Komodo dragon, and a deadly predator. Most lizards are much smaller than I am.

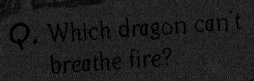

Q. Which dragon can't breathe fire?

A. The Komodo dragon!

tiny lizard!

Some types of lizard are very small. There are a few kinds of chameleon that can fit on your finger!

Pygmy chameleon

LEARN A WORD:
predator
A type of animal that hunts other animals for food.

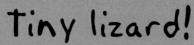

Komodo dragon

Puzzle time

Can you solve all the puzzles?

True or false?

1. Lizards are furry.
2. A basilisk lizard can run on water.
3. Some lizards eat fruit.

eggs

Can you put the letters in the right order to find four different types of egg-laying reptile?

1. NAKES
2. SAURODIN
3. ARDLIZ
4. LIDECROCO

Who gets the bug?

Only one of these chameleons can look forward to a tasty bug treat. Which one is it?

Lara

Lily

Lucy

Lost tails!

These three lizards have lost their tails. Look carefully at the patterns to match the tail to the lizard.

Larry **Lenny** **Lee**

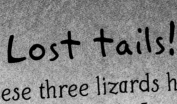

Rhyme time!

Only two of these words rhyme with "lizard." Can you find them?

tree wizard
frog splash
wash pond
mud blizzard

ANSWER: wizard, blizzard

How long am I?

Karma the chameleon's tongue is 2 inches long. His body is the same length. How long is Karma from the tip of his tongue to the tip of his tail?

ANSWER: 4 inches

What are your babies called?

My babies are called hatchlings!

They look just like me, but smaller. I don't stay with them for long after they are born. They must look after themselves.

LEARN A WORD:
hatch
When an animal, such as a lizard or bird, breaks out of its egg.

Chameleon

18

Ready to run

Hatchlings may be small,
but they are able to
run, hide, and hunt
soon after birth.

Q. How did the lizard's
egg climb a hill?
A. It scrambled up!

I look like an angry umbrella!

I puff up my neck frill as a warning to others to stay away.

Frilled lizard

Q. What do you call a reptile on a yellow brick road?
A. The lizard of Oz!

Hide and seek

This gecko has great camouflage. It looks like a dry leaf.

Leaf-tail gecko

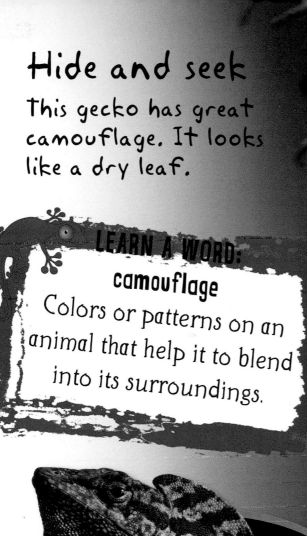

Colorful skin

Many lizards are colorful. This anole lizard's orange chin skin is called a dewlap.

21

Leon the lizard loved to play hide-and-seek in his jungle home. His green skin helped him hide among the leaves, and he could stand as still as a rock. Leon's friends would spend hours looking for him. They joked that he was an invisible lizard!

One day, Leon's friends decided it would be funny to pretend that Leon really was invisible.

Leon visited his friend Anna the snake. She was coiled up on a branch and looked asleep. "Can we play hide-and-seek?" said Leon.

"Hissssss...there's no one there," she mumbled.

"That's odd," said Leon, as he ran along the branch to find Ringo the beetle.

"Do you want to play?" Leon asked Ringo. But the black beetle scuttled past.

Leon began to feel upset. He didn't like being ignored. Then he saw Milo the monkey

swinging from a tree branch. Leon called out, "Milo, can you see me?" But Milo didn't look at Leon. He just grabbed a fig to eat.

Poor Leon! As he got angrier his skin started to change color. His tail turned blue, his body became rosy-red and his face turned yellow!

Then Scarlet the parrot swooped down next to Leon. "Wow, you look beautiful!" she said.

"I don't understand," said Leon, "why can you see me and the others can't?"

Then he heard chuckles. Leon looked around. Milo, Anna and Ringo were watching from nearby. Leon looked down at himself, and began to laugh too. No one could miss him now! As he laughed, his skin turned back to green.

"Please can we play hide-and-seek?" Leon begged.

"Of course," they said. And in a flash, Leon hid himself among the leaves once more.

By Camilla de la Bédoyère

Glossary

aboriginal a person belonging to one of the original peoples of Australia

burrow a hole or tunnel dug by a small animal

cold-blooded animals with body temperature varying with that of the environment

invisible not visible to the eye

marine of, found in, or produced by the sea

pattern a repeated decorative design

rainforest dense forest found typically in tropical areas with consistently heavy rainfall.

scales thin horny or bony plates protecting the skin of fish and reptiles

sunbathe to sit or lie in the sun

swoop move rapidly downward through the air

Websites

For web resources related to the subject of this book, go to: **www.windmillbooks.com/weblinks** and select this book's title.

Index